IMAGES
of England

HALSTEAD
AND
COLNE VALLEY

IMAGES
of England

HALSTEAD
AND
COLNE VALLEY

Compiled by
David Osborne

TEMPUS

First published 1999
Copyright © David Osborne, 1999

Tempus Publishing Limited
The Mill, Brimscombe Port,
Stroud, Gloucestershire, GL5 2QG

ISBN 0 7524 1506 9

Typesetting and origination by
Tempus Publishing Limited
Printed in Great Britain by
Midway Clark Printing, Wiltshire

Back in the busy old days when Halstead builders George Sharp were in business on Chapel Hill, Halstead. The Sharp brothers are standing in their yard, fourth from left, at the end of the cart, and first right. Their yard later became Broyd's, then the Foxearth Brewery, and is now ATS Ltd's tyre depot.

Contents

Acknowledgements

Thanks are accorded to the following for their loan of pictures, documents and general expertise:

Halstead & District Local History Society
Halstead Gazette
Percy Bamberger
Adrian Corder-Birch
Paul Downes
Ian McTaggart
Doreen Potts
Ken Stanhope
Jean Wishart

Halstead from the Public Gardens. This is an early picture of the park: many of today's huge trees are here only saplings. There appears to be a train in the station on the Colne Valley Railway from Marks Tey to Haverhill.

Introduction

There are good reasons for believing that Halstead did not become a settled community until Saxon times. There are two observations which support this. Firstly, had it been a Roman settlement or station, more indications of its occupation would have been discovered than has been the case. Secondly, it is recorded in the Domesday survey of 1086 under the distinctively Saxon name of Halsteda, only one letter's transposition away from today's form. Thirdly, it is possible to demonstrate with some degree of certainty that the village began to assume in Saxon times some of the main features of the town as it is today.

Imagine the settlement of Halstead as it may have appeared in early Norman times soon after the survey of 1086. Approach the town from the bottom of Mount Hill, below which is marshy country, badly waterlogged, stretching down to the river, and make a way along a rough pathway raised above the marsh, which turns as it nears the river and follows it until it reaches the ford by which the settlement or village is gained. Before crossing the ford, continue along the pathway where the mill of the Lord of the Manor probably stood, on the same site as the later town mill, which afterwards became part of Samuel Courtauld's factory, which itself is now but a memory.

Coming back to the ford, stepping stones allow the traveller to cross the river and pass up the main street of the village. On the left hand side, the sunny side, following the conjectured line of the modern houses, are the more pretentious dwelling places of the sockmen, or free tenants, built of timber and thatched with reeds and rushes. The survey revealed that there were twenty-two of these. In front of the houses were the gardens, stretching down to the brook which flowed down to the river, with trees and bushes growing along both sides (the route of this can be seen in some pictures in Chapter 1).

Passing up the street, one reaches the church, standing on part of the land now occupied by St Andrew's church of today. Possibly a church dedicated to St Andrew may have stood there in early Saxon times between 604 and 619. At any rate it is practically certain a church stood there at the time of the survey.

If, as is probable, the village did not extend further than the top of the High Street, it would have possible from the north side of the church to look across an open field to see the Manor of Halstead, which stood on the left side of Hedingham Road, just before the present Dog Inn. Around the village stretched the open or common field, not yet cut into the chessboard appearance of rural England today.

Soon after the Conquest, Halstead was regarded as a place of sufficient importance to be constituted as a royal market town. The market was kept on the King's Highway on Saturday after midday, and it had a pair of stocks, a pillory and an assize of bread and beer. Historian William Holman, who died in Colne Engaine church in 1730, in writing about the position of the market, says: 'Some think it was kept below town, near the bridge where on the right hand side is an open space, and where anciently stood a cross of which tradition is fresh to this day.' This space is probably that which still exists, cobbled until recently, at the bottom of the High Street in front of the houses, occupied lately by Pendle's furniture shop and the Co-op butcher's and now a restaurant and Martin's newsagents respectively.

One of the principal events in Halstead during the fifteenth and sixteenth centuries was the start of the woollen trade, which attracted what are now known as 'outworkers' who came to live in the surrounding villages, several of which began as a cottage or two around a crossing of the River Colne.

Several manorial-type houses still exist in the district today, although most have been reduced in stature to farmhouses. Some of these buildings are far removed from their original use. The fifteenth-century White Hart in the High Street once consisted of a central hall flanked by solar and buttery wings and a similar building stands on the left of Chapel Hill, now made into three dwellings.

The following century saw the rebuilding of Stansted Hall, Bois Hall (now gone) and Gladfen Hall, while a couple of miles away, Rivenhall (or Raven's) was being erected at Greenstead Green. In his *Old and New Halstead*, W.J. Evans suggested that Mr Samuel Fiske and John Morley paved the market place at their own expense in 1705. At this time, the market place was apparently moved from the bottom of the street to the site of the present fountain, where a market house once stood (this was removed in 1816).

Other benefactors in the town included William Word, who settled a house and lands called Hubbards, which provided 12s per year for the poor of the town; Dame Mary Ramsey founded a grammar school for forty free scholars within Halstead and Colne Engaine; the premises in the High Street are now occupied by the Constitutional Club. Subsequently it moved on to Earls Colne, and following another closure returned to Halstead as Ramsey School. William Martin, clothier, left lands and tenements called Coe's and Shellard's, and had what was known as a 'feoffee barn', standing on the land bounded by Martin's Road, New Street, Mitchell Avenue and Kings Road. (A feoffee was a fifth of the produce, double a tithe.)

Later, people began moving about and the old pathways became trackways for wagons and in due course, roads. Halstead, sitting on the important crossroads of the Colchester-Cambridge and Chelmsford-Bury St Edmunds roads, gradually attracted more settlers, both workers and businessmen, all looking to earn a living.

Throughout the years the villages along the valley had been growing and many of them became bigger than the original Halstead. Eventually as society in general and local government in particular became more organized, the town became the headquarters of the Halstead Union, which comprised sixteen villages when drawn up about 1876, namely: Castle and Sible Hedingham, Little and Great Yeldham, Little and Great Maplestead, Colne Engaine, Earls and White Colne, Gosfield, Pebmarsh, Ridgewell, Stambourne, Tilbury, Toppesfield and, of course, Halstead.

One
The High Street

Halstead was paid a visit by the Luftwaffe during the Second World War, at 17.42 hrs on 8 August 1940. The High Street and Parsonage Street go off the top of the picture while the Colne Valley railway goes left to Sible Hedingham and right to Earls Colne.

The ladies take the opportunity for a little window shopping before stepping into the Royal Oak, on the left, while opposite the Swan Inn's sign swings. Now Boots stands on the site.

An easy stroll at the top of the street on what appears to be on a Wednesday, for the shops have the shutters down for half-day closing. One hopes the lad with a sack on his head did not have far to go!

The High Street Congregational church, which was taken down in the 1950s. The site is now occupied by the post office. The road between the church and the old post office (off the picture to the right) is Chapel Street, once called the Rope Walk as ropes used to be made in the premises behind the church.

Further down the street is one of the first signs of mechanical transport with a motorcycle and sidecar outside Buck's the fruit and vegetable shop, later Fleet's and now a baker's shop. Note the old Co-op butcher's at the bottom of the town, now Martin's.

It is time for another chat with the two men outside Culyer's watchmakers, next to what is now John Winter Drake. Across the road the ladies are comparing ideas at Sharpley's drapery shop, known as Adelaide House in the last century and now Stead and Simpson's footwear shop.

The former Eastern Electricity showroom, above which is located The Sportsman. This was the original Town Hall, with the committee room above, from which it was rumoured that the mice used to take council business into the bar of the George Hotel next door!

A nice aerial shot from St Andrew's church tower in the early years when there were no housing estates beyond Holy Trinity church whose spire is a landmark. Older Halsteadians will remember The Common, on extreme right, where Stanley and Beridge Roads are growing.

Halfway up the street stands Gatehouse Yard, once an access to St Andrew's vicarage. Note the shop on right, George Tanswell's boot and shoe shop (No. 47), established in 1894. Robert Clarke at No. 41 was a confectioner.

At last the motor car reaches Halstead. Competing for parking spaces in those days was an unknown problem to these motorists standing opposite Henry Pountney's ironmongers and Arthur Smith's stationery and picture frame shop.

A nice quiet walk up the town, caught by the camera from St Andrew's church tower. Apart from the lack of development in Trinity parish, note the sunblind outside James Woollard's bakery and confectionery shop (No. 40), and the Manse of the Congregational church.

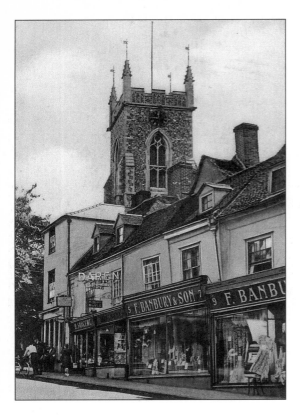

A quiet time between the wars, with Herbert Sargent's tobacconist shop (No. 3), Robert Mitchell's bakery shop (both of which once constituted the Dolphin Inn), and Frank Banbury's drapery shop, while the local constabulary talks to a cyclist outside Tom Fowler's café.

There appears to be something of interest at William Oak's grocery shop (No. 59), with several people about. On the right No. 61 was and still is Frank Smith's outfitters, while on the left were A.W. & H. Newton, who ran a smithy, latterly Chaplin & Keeble's cycle shop.

A familiar idea was to photograph the crowd of children who always gathered when the photographer turned up. Note Robert Nash's butchers shop, where Martin's now stands, while the big house on the left was William Barker's grocery shop that stood in what is now the entrance to the Solar Superstore.

A close up of Nash's butchers shop, which was followed by the Co-operative butchery. The premises were on the site of the former Guildhall, fronted by the famous cobbled area, now sadly all gone.

The once resplendent Halstead Grammar School, now the Constitutional Club, with headmaster Samuel Savery BA and his boys. In the gable brickwork on the right can be seen the letters HGS, while over the doorway of the current shop can be seen 'Get Wisdom, Forget It Not'. Back in 1594 Dame Mary Ramsey founded two grammar schools, the other being at Colne Engaine, for forty free scholars who lived within eight miles of the town. Ultimately it closed around 1908 and the boys moved to Earls Colne, the girls having their own establishment the following year in Colchester Road. Eventually it returned to Halstead as the Ramsey School in Colne Road.

An earlier shot of the Grammar School when the porchway was thatched, before the rebuilding. Note the board between the windows with the story of the founding of the school; this can now be seen at the current Ramsey School.

A quiet day at the top of the street in around 1887 when the obelisk erected for Queen Victoria's Jubilee stood on the site of the fountain. Note that the former three-storey Doubleday's grocery shop now has only two floors and St Andrew's church boasts impressive double gates.

A later shot of a similar location. The Beehive tobacconist's was still in business until recent years, while Herbert Sargent's bakery became Robert Mitchell's and when Frank Banbury took over the next-door properties, the Simmons brothers moved down beside the town bridge.

A common enough shot of the street, once again with a noticeable lack of traffic in this peaceful scene. Note the awning outside Adelaide House, a draper's, while the empty wagon opposite has no horse: perhaps the driver is in the Royal Oak for lunch!

The traffic curse hit Halstead between the wars and here it looks quite crowded, although there is no need for car parks yet. Note the dustcart outside what is now Barclays Bank. If any of these vehicles still survive today, what would they be worth?

A peaceful scene looking down the hill with very few people about. This postcard was published by Barry & Co. who traded at No. 21, who in turn was followed by Maurie Hunt's sweet shop/ice cream parlour, and is now The Card Shop.

Halstead Post Office, built in 1895 when Henry Lake Hughes was the postmaster. It was used as a furniture shop, pet shop and now a keep fit establishment, when the new post office was built next door, on the site of the old High Street Congregational Church.

Looking from St Andrew's church tower when North Street (Hedingham Road) was much narrower, with the London & County Bank on the corner. Very little has been built on The Common in the background, better known as Beridge and Stanley Roads.

A close-up of the same premises. The London & County Bank was involved with Sparrow and Tufnell, bankers, and eventually became Barclays Bank, now further down the street. Sparrow's Pond recalls the same family.

Back to the tower for a more modern look, when the bank premises were demolished to widen the road, with shrubs established on most of the site. Note the football ground in the far centre, indicating the photograph was taken around 1950 when the stand was built.

23

Long a landmark in the Halstead skyline, St Andrew's church, whose registers date from 1564 and whose bells were cast in 1573, had attractive double gates, long since gone. The splendid copper beech tree, here but a sapling, is also well known.

In the lower part of the street in the early years of this century stood Adelaide House, (then a drapery), George Culyer's newspaper shop (No. 85), a private house, then Tom Miller's fried fish shop. All were taken down in the 1920s and the site now forms part of the Co-operative Stores.

Halstead High Street, wreathed in a mantle of snow, but with no traffic stuck on the hill. One or two sad souls are in evidence, while the others might be in the Swan (right) or Royal Oak (left), far warmer places in this weather!

This shot looks quite a common view down the High Street, but a close study reveals that the former post office has not yet been built, thus making it prior to 1895. At that time Henry Lake Hughes was postmaster in a small house that stood on the same site.

This is a commonly photographed view from the top of the High Street, here from before 1907 when the Three Crowns closed down (Archie Woolf was its proprietor). It stood on the site of the present motor dealers; the pub sign is still legible in the plaster work between the right and centre windows.

Two
Round the Town

A nice aerial shot of the town in 1950 with the A131 snaking from Head Street at the bottom to Mount Hill at the top. Samuel Courtauld's factory is prominent at the top. A closer look sees the old St Andrew's School (centre left) and the centre bottom recalls the time when Halstead had two water towers. The empty spaces around town bear witness to the many housing developments that now cover them.

A stroll around during the winter when the photographer found himself at Parsonage Street bridge looking towards the town with the old Courtauld powerhouse beyond the trees. The building on the left was once the Co-operative bakery.

It must have been a bit like heaven in the old days in Sudbury Road, with just one car and a motorcycle in view as the lonely wagon clip-clops its way out of town opposite the junction with Colne Road.

Quieter times before the First World War down Pump Yard off Hedingham Road, which used to run parallel with Belle Vue. Barely visible at the road end is the former Rising Sun public house which closed in 1907, becoming in turn a fish and chip shop then a baker's.

This picture of Crowbridge in around 1910 is startlingly different from today's view. A policeman still had time for a word before another wagon enters town. The fields in the background are now built on, while the house on the right has long gone.

The changing face of Head Street: these cottages used to stand close to the now closed Rose and Crown. The top one (No. 38) was Mrs Sylvia Roberts' confectionery shop just before the last war, then Kennet's pet shop for a spell.

Again the people come out to welcome the photographer at the top of Mount Hill. The cottage on the left bounded a footpath across what is now the bottom of Blamsters Crescent to the top of Mount Pleasant. On the left were the Blamster's Farm workers' cottages.

A bird's eye view of St Andrew's crossroads at the top of the High Street, with the Chira-Diagnostics works (formerly Evans' Electro) just beyond the trees. The now closed United Reformed church still has its steeple, while the newly built Baptist church in Hedingham Road has the inevitable car park next door.

This old doorway was found in property demolished about 1920 to make way for the Jane Austen houses built by Samuel Courtauld in Hedingham Road. It is believed to be part of the original manor house of Abel St Martin.

Again the children become an audience at the Head Street-Colchester Road junction where they would not dare stand today. Ernest Brazier's wirework shop on the right appears to be a popular notice board, with the office of Stanley Moger's auctioneers next door.

A view from the days when Samuel Courtauld's factory was one of the two biggest employers in town; it has now been replaced by the giant Solar Superstore. Relatively modern premises include the Electric Motor Development, industrial units at the rear of the former factory powerhouse, the Precinct in the High Street, and the housing area at Park Drive, off Mitchell Avenue.

A favourite view up Trinity Street, bordered by the horse chestnuts, now sadly gone. This was taken before 1907, the year the Railway Bell closed down. It was demolished and replaced by the cinema and is now a Chinese takeaway.

A view in the other direction, towards town, certainly much earlier judging by the smaller trees alongside the Recreation Ground. Note that the post box outside the then Adam's Brewery has moved across the road. The men with the ladder would step lively these days!

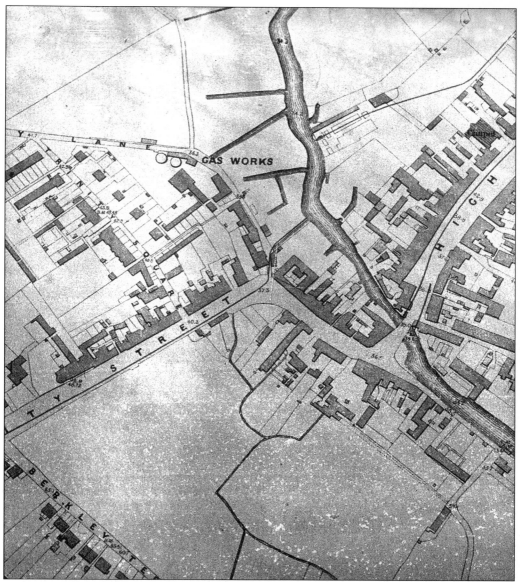

One of the early street maps shows Berkeley Terrace (bottom left), where a Mrs Berkeley ran a dame school around 1855. It was previously called Prospect Terrace and is now New Street. Note there is no Kings Road: Rosemary Lane runs off to Slough Farm and there is no railway line in sight. Thus the map is prior to 1860.

A different view of Bridge Street, in the days of Harry Newton's blacksmiths (to the right), later Mellon's DIY store; Baldry & Walker's fish and chip shop; Sollie Brewer's bookies (Symond's grocery); Crown Café (Albert Newton's greengrocery/wet fish shop and The Brick pub, later Charles' Bakery) and the Railway Hotel.

A special house on Chapel Hill, Rose Cottage, the inside part being the first home of the author. Originally Mrs Priscilla Lightfoot lived there, the widow of Revd Taylor Lightfoot, minister of the New Street Methodist church. Rose Cottage was demolished around 1970.

Edward Argent used to trade as a tailor and sold 'clothes for the working man' opposite the Bull Hotel, before Harry Newton took over as blacksmith. Note in the background the iron railing fence round the station yard.

The former Clover's Mill in Bridge Street, now the empty Wisebuy's store. This was a building of some note: it was once the town jail and headquarters of the North Hinckford Police Division from 1840 until the current police station was built in 1851 in Trinity Street.

The last days of Summer's Row, *c.* 1980 – just off Mount Pleasant, next to the now closed Carpenter's Arms. Originally called Cook's Row, it was built around 1850 by Mr William Cook, who was responsible for several other housing areas in Halstead.

Mount Pleasant looks a little tatty in the early years of the century despite being built in 1850. On the extreme left is Last's, then Cracknell's general stores (No. 14), which was a very busy little shop for years, but converted to a residence about twenty-five years ago.

A tranquil scene in Bridge Street. From the left the shops are: Henry Potter, herbalist and yeast dealer and sub post-office; Ted Doe's butchers shop (a 'British Restaurant' during the Second World War); and the smaller Co-op building, which was demolished to extend the premises in 1924.

The old town bridge, built in 1846, has undergone two replacements since. Barker's grocery shop stands on the right, while to the left there seems to be a bit of sign-writing on London House, the drapery establishment of William Exinor Dunt (later to become Simmons Bros before being closed).

A closer look at the old blacksmith's shop in Bridge Street. This was run by Harry Newton, whose predecessors A.W. & H. Newton ran a smithy in 57 High Street before moving down the hill around 1910. Earlier an outfitter's shop, Edward Argent's, stood on the site. William George Dunt opened his linen and drapery shop at London House next door, after leaving his father's (William Charles') shop in Trinity Street. At the time of the closure Simmons Bros ran the establishment after moving down from the High Street around 1928.

Another nice aerial shot taken prior to 1950, dated by the lack of a stand at the Town football ground, top left. Note the line across the pitch indicating where the old stream ran, while the darker patch in the top penalty area showed the location of a former sandpit. The arrow-shaped piece of land behind the bottom goal, and that beyond it down to the river, is now part of the Broton Industrial Estate. These were the days when an allotment was a necessity, as seen at The Moys, on the left of Hedingham Road and those around the United Reformed church in Parsonage Street. Also of interest is Charlie Bragg's winkle shop (with sunblind) at the junction of Hedingham Road and Upper Chapel Street.

A look down Sloe Hill towards town in winter, with Holy Trinity church spire just visible on the extreme left. The large house in the centre has long gone, but beyond the roof line can be seen chimneys of some of the first houses in Beridge Road, around the turn of the century.

A view in the other direction towards Gosfield with The Plantation on the left, where in wartime stood several Nissen huts for personnel who worked at Sloe House. This was then a military HQ, but had once been home to Robert Greenwood, a town worthy, founder of the Halstead Gas Company.

A smart lady stands on the steps of Wellesley House, in Colchester Road. Note the lime tree standing on the edge of the path, once a feature of the town and copied along other roads.

Brazier's wireworks establishment, with Stanley Moger's office displaying posters next door. Further up the hill on the right, past the wagon, is Ernest Knight's hardware shop, while on the left is Ernest Rowland's hairdressing shop (No. 14).

Simply a beautiful, tranquil scene near Star Stile House, typical of the Colne Valley.

An etching of the old Baptist church and Manse in Hedingham Road, seen in the days of Queen Victoria. By the number of people in the picture walking towards the gate, it appears they are about to attend a service.

Approximately the same location in 1950 when the old Manse was still standing. Beyond the car was John Harvey's saddlery and leather shop, and behind the car were Frank Airey's tea rooms and sweet shop. Remember the fizzy drinks for a penny down the slide?

A quiet spot in Hedingham Road almost opposite Box Mill Lane. These cottages were removed in the 1920s when Samuel Courtauld, who lived at The Howe, built his Jane Austen houses towards the town, as well as others in Colchester Road and Mallows Field.

Halstead Workhouse in Hedingham Road, built in 1848 for 250 inmates at a cost of £7,500, was pulled down in 1922 to make way for the Homes of Rest. It was replaced by Samuel Courtauld as part of his benefice to the town and built by Messrs Deaves of Bures.

An idyllic setting of the former Lodge House of The Howe in around 1910. The Howe was the home of Samuel Courtauld, whose father George used to live at Mill House, in the Causeway, next to his factory, which was one of the seeds of the giant textile industry.

DOE'S CORNER
(Nº 4.)
HALSTEAD

Doe's Corner, Hedingham Road, in much quieter days. These cottages have long gone – they disappeared to enable the road to be widened for the increasing traffic just after the First World War. To the right is Fitzjohns and Dynes Hall.

Weavers Row looks very similar today, but in fact these cottages stood next to the present row and were demolished prior to the building of Harvey Street in 1934. The land up to the hedge fronting them was a smallholding belonging to Arthur Osborne, landlord of The Globe.

Brook Farm, Colchester Road, in the days when the busy A604 was just a quiet road to Earls Colne and Colchester. It was the home of a Miss Williams in the early years of the century, when this picture was taken.

St Andrew's church stands supreme, with no damage to the churchyard wall. Note on the left the office of Mr Stanley Moger, the Halstead businessman who was involved in almost every town activity for many years.

At one time Halstead boasted a Salvation Army Citadel in Parsonage Street opposite the former White Horse. In its time it housed Tom Keneally's film shows and was once Thomas Moy's accounts office but is now the Masonic Hall.

The last remains of a prominent house in Sudbury Road, Bois Hall, which stood in Halstead for 200 years. It was the home of Mr Harry Portway for some years around the turn of the century, while Land Army girls were based there in the last war.

Three
At Play

In the days when paddling was a popular pastime, children used to play at Blue Bridge, Colchester Road. At one time the river bed was covered by boards, which were possibly for the children's benefit and still remained until recent years.

After the last war, Halstead people were keen to get back to relaxing and playing again, or simply having fun, even though it was still a time of rationing. However, they soon organized themselves into various societies and found time for the Town Carnival and Procession in 1948. The lady pushing her bicycle behind the 'nurses' is Mrs Grace Page, of Mount Pleasant, who played the piano at hundreds of parties through the years.

St Andrew's Sunday school in around 1947, including: Barbara Jeggo, Beulah Everett, Betty Tanswell, Cecily Reeve, Wendy Runtle, Jill Marsh, Joan Wicker, Pat Bayliss, Beryl Maskell, Doreen Sutton, Berys Radford, Jean Ward, Elizabeth Drury, Barbara Ward, Betty Bullen, Jill Osborne, Margaret Rayner, Hilary Chapman, Brigitte Bearman, Edna Barrett, Ruth Bearman, Janet Cook and Elizabeth Dearman.

The Pirates of Penzance, staged by St Andrew's Boys' Club, *c.* 1920. From left to right, back row: Ted Butcher, Charlie Warner, Horace Edwards, Ernie Edwards, Frank Vaizey, George Green, Fred Warren, Olive Matthews. Front row: 'Mun' Harvey, Alf Wicker, Helen Pullen, Tom Hampton.

It's been a long, long time since the River Colne froze over hard enough for these ice skating activities near the Chapel Street bridge looking towards Hedingham. The picture is probably from 1947, the winter of the big freeze.

There appears to be something to celebrate in the yard of the Greenwood School, Head Street; the reason has been a puzzle for years. Yet again the photographer, rather than the sandwiches, draws the attention of the children!

Halstead Empire was used by St Andrew's Boys' Club in 1919. From left to right, back row: G. Mayes, W. Harvey, Charlie Stubbings, Fred Suckling, Harold Goodrum, Cyril Warner, Sid Symonds, Frank Rayner, Charlie Warner, Bert Evans, E. Nash, E. Clark, H. Harboard, A. Clark. Second row: Alf Wicker, E. Walford, I. Winterflood, Ivy Beckwith, F. Newman, Morton Brazier, E. Wicks, Edward Lindekam, M. Goodrum, L. Hunt, C. Byford, C. Ward, Will Dunt. Third row: Frank Norman, B. Coe, M. Maurice, C. Porter, Eric Webber, Bert Staines, Basil Staines. Front row: A. Drury, D. Danby, A. Stubbings, F. Barker and Gerald Brazier.

The employees of Adams Brewery of Halstead enjoyed a charabanc trip to the Empire Exhibition at Wembley in 1924, but judging by the solid tyres just visible it must have been a bumpy ride! Seated fourth from the right in front is Bill Patmore. Can any one else be identified?

The Halstead Gala committee of 1894. From left to right, back row: William Sheen, Dr Roberts, Will Turnell, Ernie Potter, W. Drane, Will Errington, J. French, Walter Yerbury, Tom Bate. Front: O. Kemp, Edw. Smith, Harry Portway, Francis Harris, Revd J. Andrews, Arthur Kibble, Frank Wallis.

The East Essex Hunt used to meet at Halstead on Boxing Day. The former town jail, latterly Clover's Mill, is on the right; Buck's carriage works is next to the Co-op on the left, yet to be extended. Arthur Doe, later son Ted's butchers shop, at the extreme left, is now a bookies.

The 4th Halstead Scouts celebrate at the 1950 Christmas party. Taking part are: John Juniper, John Newell, Brian Fitz, George Layer and Tony George (scout masters, centre with scarf and woggle); John Wiseman, Brian Richmond, 'Copper' Clark, Mick Francis, Paul Redman, Mervyn Redman, Billy Redman, Ralph Wilkin, Roger Potter, Arthur Wicks, Robert Lake, Gilbert Lake, David Diss, Roger Smith, Lynn Brown, Larry Plumb, Derek Kibble, Laurie Sullivan, Denny Turner, George Ashby, Bobby Felton, Peter Earey, Billy Cook. Helpers: Mrs Redman, Mrs Lake, Mrs Felton, Mrs Margie Smith, Mrs Turner, Mrs Potter, Mrs Gwen Hardy, Audrey Porter, Margery Allen and Marshall Wicks.

A trio of 'clowns' on parade, from left to right: Claude Byford, Alf Wicker and Bert Meadows. They were all members of St Andrew's Boys' Club in the 1920s, who often played their part in various entertainments for the townsfolk.

An excursion on the train was an exceptional day out for Halstead people soon after the First World War, and the annual Co-operative Society trip to Clacton attracted large crowds for the biggest day of the year for many. This occasion was in 1924, when hats were a must!

The Coronation of King George V brought out the crowds to celebrate at the top of the High Street where the people are all dressed in their Sunday best for the occasion. Doubleday's grocery shop is on right, with the George Hotel (now Lloyds Bank) on the left. In the centre is the one-time Town Hall, later the Mechanics and Literary Institute, the forerunner of the present-day library. Note the 'chosen few' on the top floor for a better view of the celebrations, and the sign of the Three Crowns on the right, which closed before the First World War.

The Hedingham Road Baptist church, shows several hirsute gentlemen among those who took their Male Bible Class very seriously when this photograph was taken on 13 August 1879, when Revd Edmund Morley was the minister.

The Boys' Brigade of St Andrew's Boys' Club, complete with pillbox hats, with their leader Mr Frank A. Vaizey, seventh from the left in the middle row. In those days many young men of Halstead belonged to a variety of institutions, thus keeping out of mischief.

Four

At School

Class III pupils at Holy Trinity at the turn of the century look rather bewildered for probably their first picture. Pinafores seem to be the vogue for the girls, while boots are the order of the day for the boys. The lady in the doorway is possibly Miss Ada Hutchings, the infants' teacher.

Time for Class I of Holy Trinity in 1917 to step forward. From left to right, back row: Miss Glasson, Freda Cook, Mary Norfolk, Reg Palmer, Effie Allen, Revd Albert Austin, Bob Clift, -?-, Miss Ethel Spurgeon. Centre row: Ernie Boreham, Hilda Miller, Violet Harding, Les Runtle, Lily Rulton, Ron Rayner, Jack Rulton, Ernie Pilgrim, Jack Mills, Jack Hardy. Front row : Edith Johnson, Ethel Rayner, Catherine Ives, Mary Smith, Audrey Saunders, Florrie Smith, Eva Coote, Maisie Vitler, Winnie Grunwell, Ernie Daines.

Holy Trinity in 1931. From left to right, back row: Mrs Frimley (headmistress), Jeff Davis, Edwin Heavingham, Cliff Sudbury, Ovilliers Fenner, Geoff Griffiths, George Pagington, Don Abbott, George Pudney, Edwin Grunwell, Len Bragg. Second row: Bobby Broyd, Tony Rayner, Edna Broyd, Nola Claydon (half hidden), Joan Smith, Ruby Rayner, Velda Fenner, Phyllis Grunwell, Jill Miller, Muriel Heavingham, Violet Tofts, Sadie Pettitt. Third row: Ruby Bearman, Lily Finch, Grace Hart, Iris Sach, Doris Cooper, Olive Akers, Poppy Jeggo, Dorothy Barber, Peggy Coote, Eileen Hume, Peter Cook, Brian Bush, Revd Albert Austin, Peter Newton. Front row: Doug Spurgeon, George Root, Ernie Pilgrim, Jack Andrews, Eunice Wordsworth, Kath Pye, Iris Smith, Joan Robinson, Olive Meadows, Brenda Chumbley, Ella Eary, Joan Herbert, Lewis Sewell, Gordon Carter and Noel Downs.

Holy Trinity Lower School in 1903, when Miss Alice Rudd was headmistress. This school was situated on Tidings Hill and was founded around 1868; it is now a private house standing, predictably, in School Chase. From left to right, back row: Miss Sims (teacher), ? Goodey, ? Goodey, Nora Norman, Nettie Norman, Lil Parker, Edie Parker, -?-. Second row: -?-, Jack Root, ? Smith, Jenny Bowles, ? Smith, Fred Parker, ? Smith, Stan Norman, -?-. Third row: May Root, -?-, Ruth Bowles, Billy Bowles, Annie Root, Alice Root, Minnie Hall, Dolly Parker, Rhoda Parker, -?-. Front row: Gordon Norman, Cecil Norman, -?-, Reg Kibble, Alice Cansell, Hilda Harrington and Hettie Harrington.

Halstead Girls' Grammar School in Colchester Road, which is now part of Ramsey School. These are the prefects in 1927. From left to right, back row: Dorothy Creswell, Evelyn Doe, Margaret Hill, Joan Pearson. Centre row: Carrie Barrell, Freda Mortimer, Nora Barry, Phyllis Root. Front row: Olive Jay and Gladys Spinks.

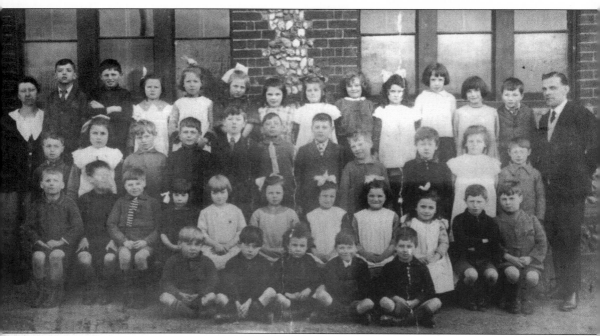

St Andrew's School, *c.* 1923. Included in the back row are: ? Evans, Eric Webber, Joyce Cranfield, Joan Deal, Muriel Danby, ? Evans, Minnie Root, Billy Edwards. In the middle row: Hilda Goodey, Frank Mead, Una Clark, Charlie Clift. Front row: Hedley Iron, Sheila Collier, May Clark, Frank Gladwell. Can anyone fill in the blanks?

Halstead Council School in 1919. Among those identified are the headmaster Mr Morton Mathews, teacher Miss Daisy Taylor and some of the girls: Lily Potter, Susan Outing, Kate Coppin, Norah Lee, Lily Rulton, May Mead, Hilda Parker, Elsie Burst, Edie Borman.

St Andrew's senior pupils line up in the late 1920s. From left to right, back row: Eddie Barker, Beat Kimber, Kath Cranfield, Hilda Dorking, Phyllis Smith, Gwen Pogson, Hilda Miller, Win Goodram, Iris Danby, Stan Whitfield. Second row: Fred Kibble, Jack Hostler, Eddie Evans, Stan Tyson, Margery Webber, Abigail Hills, Annie Evans, Ted Amos, Denny Ostler, Johnny Curtis, Bob Goward. Third row: Geoff Whitfield, Jack Mills, Eric Webber, Marjorie Norman, Mr E. Walford, Ivy Dorking, Ethel Mills, Marshall Wicks, Les Gould, Doug Baker. Front row: Bert Goodey, Jimmy Goodey and Bill Miller.

Halstead Council School infants in the early 1920s. From left to right, back row: -?-, Miss Newton, Miss Gertrude Wadley (headmistress). Second row: Vic Coe, -?-, Will Cook, -?-, Cyril Pilgrim, Dennis Rayner, George Abrams, Percy Catley, ? Byford, -?-. Third row: Margaret Pingo, Lily Cracknell, Phyllis Smith, Ethel Outing, Milly Burl, Vera Townsend, Rene Wicker. Front row: Les Daines, Jack Darling, -?-, -?-, George Nicholls, Herby Finch, Arthur Chaplin, Bert Smith, Cecil Constable.

Halstead Council School infants' class, 1937. From left to right, back row: Miss Carpenter, Terry Bragg, Ronnie Gurteen, Keith Lee, Neal Rayner, -?-, Bobby Ellis, Ray Norman. Centre row: Molly Sayward, Rita Harvey, Francis Rayner, Valerie Fowler, Audrey Porter, Pam Dollin. Front row: Peter Diss, Beulah Williamson and Freddie Amos.

Halstead Infants' School, *c*. 1912. From left to right, back row: Miss Dora Pudney (headmistress), -?-, George Bonnett, -?-, Sid Root, Miss Newton. Second row: Len Hardy, Hurrell Rayner, Bert Miller, Arthur Williamson, Cecil Beckwith, Eb Norman, -?-, ? Wicker, -?-, Sam Hermon, -?-, Ted Taylor, George Ashard. Third row: -?-, -?-, May Amey, Blanche Smith, ? Harding, Doris Bartholomew, Lil Whitehead, Madge Dixey, Rose Drury, Hilda Newton, Win Osborne, Doris Coe, Rene Runtle. Front row: -?-, -?-, -?-, Lil Sharman, Doris Porter, Violet Binks, Doris Sewell, -?-, Emily Clarke, Harold Runtle.

Class II of Holy Trinity in 1900. Back row: Sid Taylor, H. Spurgeon, Fred Mayes, P. Paveley, P. Cook, H. Goodchild, A. Prior, M. Sargent, R. Beadle, B. Everett, S. Tokeley, F. Chapman, D. Hart. Centre row: B. Smith, ? Finch, E. Spurgeon, E. Parsley, D. Harrington, F. Reeve, E. Fletcher, E. Smith, Percy Bush, D. Hart, M. Root. Front row: E. Norman, ? Finch, A. Wells, E. Diss, Beat Gaymer, B. Wells, Sid Symonds, N. White. (The little boy behind the front row is unknown.)

Halstead Council School Class VII boys, 1922. From left to right, back row: Morton Mathews, Miss Moore. Second row: ? Digby, ? Preston, ? Warren, Reg Wishart, ? Buck, ? Phillips, ? Boreham. Third row: ? Rayner, ? Warren, -?-, ? Bridge, ? Dean, Charlie Tempan, Ted Nichols, Arthur Bugbee. Front row: ? Wilkin, ? Tibble, ? Daines, ? Copsey, ? Argent, ? Jennings and ? Thompson.

Halstead Council School boys in the early 1920s. From left to right, back row: Teddy Baker (teacher), Eddie Alston, Spencer Copsey, Tom Mayes, R. Rayner, Reg Gaymer, Morton Mathews (headmaster), D. Newton, R. Constable, R. Wyatt, Aubrey Kemp, T. Livermore. Centre row: T. Tempan, W. Carter, F. Havers, F. Warren, A. Daines, Fred Backler, L. Brown, Jack Potter, R. Plumb, M. Kibble. Front row: J. Joyce, Ted Nichols, A. Hockley, Herschel Kibble, Bert Amey, ? Hockley, Arthur Bugbee.

St Andrew's School, Class III, *c.* 1933. From left to right, back row: Mr E. Walford, Edna Shuttleworth, Winnie Finch, ? Brooks, Edie Bocking. Second row: ? Abbott, ? Offord, Jack Tansley, Will Argent, George Sycamore, ? Brooks. Third row: Dora Wicker, Beat Draper, Florrie Abbott, ? Kemp, ? Abbott, May Diss, Doris Gardiner. Front row: ? Offord, ? Rulton, Hazel Bragg, Arthur Keeble, Jack Hostler, George Cousins, ? Goodey and Frankie Harrington.

St Andrew's School boys, *c.* 1910. From left to right, back row: ? Sheen, ? Tyler, C. Gibbs, M. Poole, H. Wiffin, S. Gladwell, ? Rivells, W. Eves, A. Rayner, B. Hawkes. Centre row: R. Andrews, S. Curtis, A. Spinks, ? Rivells, E. Wicker, ? Catchpole, ? Marven, F. Wiffin, J. Weston. Front: ? Davey, B. Basham, R. Wiffen, Redvers Ardley, P. Brown, ? Amos, J. Bullard, -?-, ? Miller, R. Patrick.

St Andrew's School boys, *c.* 1912. Back row: ? Snowdon, Bob Cooper, Reg Anderson, -?-, Harry Parsons, Percy Cook, -?-. Centre row: Lou Gladwell, Alf Edwards, Len Ward, -?-, Baden Marsh, Bert Warren, Aubrey Goodey, Albert Wiffin, Fred Coe. Front row: Don Brown, -?-, Redvers Ardley, Bert Brewer, Cecil Debenham, Hubert Brooks and Arthur Maskell.

St Andrew's School boys, 1916. From left to right, back row: 'Lolly' Clarry, Billy Emberson, Fred Mayes, Dick Sly, Reg Tansley, Charlie Stubbings, Miss Timbruss. Second row: Sid Constable, Percy Ward, Bert Rulton, Fred Amos, Nat Evans, Frank Norman, Cyril Warner, Miss Timbruss. Third row: -?-, -?-, -?-, Alf Argent, Bert Staines, Horace Wicker, Ted Suckling. Fourth row: Jack Clements, Jack Argent, Eddie Cook, Dick Harrington, Fred Warren, Chris Danby, Alf Corder. Front row: Gerald Brazier, Ted Webber, Alan Cottis, ? Norris, Dick Coe.

Five

At Work

Christmas 1952 in Halstead Post Office was busy with festive mail, but this is a small amount compared to the quantity these days. The sorters are, from left to right: -?-, Brian Firmin, Albert Cross, Lew Everett, Rene Cross, Eric Firmin, 'Tubby' Warren and an unknown girl.

It's over thirty years since Halstead railway station was in business, as seen from the former Newgrain silo. The line came to the town in 1861 and lasted almost a century. The building on the lower right housed the workshops in the days of the Colne Valley Railway, but when the LNER took over, bigger engine sheds and the freight depot were moved to the other side of the line. Readers will doubtless remember the large advertising hoarding that stood at the junction of Kings Road and Trinity Street, now Gozzett's petrol station, while the rest of the yard is now housing and the EMD factory.

Little delivery vans were the vogue between the wars. This one belonged to Jimmy Norton who ran the Beehive tobacconist's shop at 2 High Street (his son was the builder). The driver is Stan Runtle, his young brother Basil, his assistant, sitting on the running board.

Milk deliveries in town were mostly by John Surrey, from Crowbridge Farm. Milk was dispensed in a jug from the churns transported on a pony and trap and here in New Street a call is made to John 'Pills' Taylor, at No. 40.

The Tortoise Foundry was the biggest employer of men in Halstead, and here the men, mostly moulders and coremakers, line up, *c.* 1912 – see the key below: 1. Arthur 'Silver' Root; 2. Charlie Halls; 3. Charlie Turp; 4. Frank 'Ichabod' Rowland; 5. Harry 'Hutchy' Beckwith; 6. Herbert 'Steady Pin' Beckwith; 7. ? Diss; 8. 'Wawya' Kemp; 9. Ted Potter; 10. Ted Brown; 11. George Gordon. 12. Arthur Wicker; 13. Jack Howlett; 14. Fred Cook; 15. Fred Stammers; 16. Lew Bearman; 17. Herb Heavingham; 18. Walter 'Stumbler' Smith; 19. Bert Daw; 20. Fred Shelley; 21. Jim Humphries; 22. 'Arpy' Sayward; 23. 'Apenny' Potter; 24. George 'Doubler' Heavingham; 25. George Graham; 26. ? Gladden; 27. Charlie Conway; 28. Arthur Cook; 29. Sid Beckwith; 30. 'Soopy' Root; 31. Ted Norman; 32. Arthur Plumb; 33. Fred Heavingham; 34. Arthur Parmenter; 35. Lou Everett; 36. Percy Brazier; 37. Charlie Warner; 38. Arthur Burst; 39. Jim Diss; 40. Jimmy Sewell; 41. George Gaymer; 42. Bertie 'Pills' Francis; 43. Tom Francis; 44. Percy Warner; 45. Percy Francis; 46. Alf 'Donnix' Sycamore; 47. Jimmy Springett; 48. Herb 'Chick' Wright; 49. Percy Williamson; 50. Arthur 'Fibbun' Osborne (author's grandfather); 51. George 'Putt' Lee; 52. 'Buller' Staines; 53. George 'Hettie' Osborne; 54. Len Amos; 55. Arthur Sayward; 56. Bob Mills; 57. 'Pimmy' Hunt; 58. (in window) Fred Lee.

In the days of the railway, coals used to be delivered round town in horse and cart by Thomas Moy, of Kings Road. It was a big day when they switched to motor transport. These are, from left to right: Ernie Pettitt, Tom Fletcher, Maurice Kemp, Percy Warren, Billy Martin, -?-, George Stock.

It appears to be early in the century when Halstead Co-operative Society was delivering bread in Stanley Road. The driver was a Mr Cook, while his lad, Albert Warner, went on to be a departmental manager in later years.

Should such a scene grace the High Street these days, Halstead would come to a standstill! Back in 1904 Samuel Courtauld's factory was due to have a new steam boiler to replace their gas power at the powerhouse along Factory Terrace.

The boiler arrived by rail from the north of England and was towed from the station by Mark Gentry's steam engine. It has drawn great crowds of townsfolk as it approaches The Clippers, as Factory Terrace was called in those days.

Negotiating this turn was a work of art, but it eventually made it. Over the years the powerhouse became the works canteen. The site was marked by an arch in the present Solar car park and a new powerhouse was built in the Causeway, now used by Maycast-Nokes.

A stroll along the Causeway at the time of this picture would reveal a Courtauld's chimney that used to be at the blacksmith's (now tea rooms). What is now the British Legion used to be the factory canteen, as the inscription above the front door suggests.

Albie Lawrence was a legend in his time as a Halstead baker from 14 Trinity Square, now called Butler Road. Portway's foundry, behind him, was a very valued customer for his famous pads. The shop was demolished a few years ago, but is now being re-built.

For more than 150 years, Charles Portway and subsequent family members have been in business in Halstead as ironmongers. The world-famous Tortoise Stoves provided the main production in the 1930s.

Halstead Tanyard is no more. It stood in the Chapel Street car park; this shot was taken from the old Co-op car park back in the 1950s. Hugh Brown & Co.'s establishment actually operated from 52 High Street (the front door) for nearly fifty years.

The George Hotel, with some of the staff outside, including the pony and trap that met the trains. It was first mentioned in an 1839 directory, but may have been renamed. It eventually closed around 1909 and is now Lloyds Bank.

Albert Chaplin was regularly seen around town on his bike, possibly on a test run from Chaplin & Keeble's cycle shop at 57 High Street, which traded from there from 1903. It was a pleasant ride in those days! The premises are still used as a cycle and motoring spares shop.

One has to look long and hard to find a traditional farrier these days, but years back every locality had one or more. Above is Alf Bearham who ran the smithy in Head Street, which stood behind the veterinary surgeon's premises at No. 38.

It was the normal practice for many in the last century to mend footware at home, although the local 'snob' was in great demand, and here is one such man, John Bragg, who lived at No. 1 Highbury Terrace from about 1892 until 1903.

The Town Crier was a man of some renown in the old days and no exception was 'Rocky' Bragg of Halstead (in the bowler hat). He announced the news and appeared to collect children on his rounds near The Wash, Hedingham Road, attracted by gifts of fruit.

A scene from the time when Samuel Courtauld's factory was in full production. Here is weaver Flo Rayner on her Butterworth & Dickinson jacquard loom, with overseer Bert Brewer ready to remedy any problems.

Another look at Courtauld's, here on its Open Day. Paul Williamson, centre, explains to the visitors what operator Vi Slaughter is doing with slaying rods on a warp. In latter years the Czechoslovakian water jet looms made this process out of date.

A nostalgic walk round the old factory for three former employees. Left is Fred Brown, foreman on the spooling, Fred Baker, who worked in card-cutting and Mrs Hilda Morley of the canteen, with the original tea trolley she used to push round the various departments. It seems impossible for such a busy establishment to have completely gone after trading in Halstead since the 1840s; but it has been replaced by the Solar Superstore.

One of Halstead's old-time shopkeepers, Stanley Symonds, who ran his grocery shop in Bridge Street from the early 1930s until its closure. Afterwards it became Solly Brewer's betting shop. All the shops have now gone to be replaced by the modern complex.

This is not strictly a 'working' picture, but so many people from Trinity parish used the old railway bridge to walk to work at Courtauld's or go shopping up the High Street that it merits inclusion. This shot was taken in 1920, before the Second World War scrap metal drive claimed railings around gardens.

Six
At Events

The Proclamation of Queen Elizabeth II in 1952 is read out from the fountain by Stanley Symonds, chairman of Halstead UDC. From left to right: Edward Lindekam, -?-, Ronald Long, Jack Root, Evelyn Brown, Ted Parker, John Frost and 'Mun' Harvey.

The Tythings was the setting back in the 1960s for Mayor John Frost officially to plant a tree, watched by councillors Geoffrey Waterer, Edward Hodgkinson, Ronald Long and Ted Parker, along with members of the Co-operative Society.

The weekly Halstead market was the place to be on a Tuesday in years gone by. It was held in Colchester Road, on a site behind the Woodman Inn. Livestock was sold until 1939 but the market eventually dwindled to furniture, tools etc. before closure in the 1960s.

One of the most important items of Halstead heritage was the Co-op clock used by thousands of people over the years to check on both trains and buses across the road. It was unveiled at the 1935 Silver Jubilee which attracted a large crowd.

A milestone in the history of the former Halstead Urban District Council was the opening of the new offices in Red House, Colchester Road, in 1936 by the Rt Hon. R.A. Butler MP (in the centre of the doorway). From left to right: Harry Hughes, Charlie Sewell, Fred Plaistow, Fred Cocksedge, Harry Sturmer, Bob Minter, Will Knowles, behind is Stanley Moger, Sam Pye (chairman), R.A. Butler, Will Nicholson (surveyor), Dr John Ranson (MoH), in front Ronald Long (clerk), Ted Parker, Bert Lock, Charlie Ready, Francis Adams, Cyril Nash, Kerr Vaizey, Mrs Nash and George Clark, council foreman and chief of the fire brigade.

The Coronation of King George V was enjoyed by the people of the town with celebrations on the Market Hill. The venue was suitably decorated for the occasion while the people had on their Sunday best, especially the ladies with their splendid hats.

The floods of 1947 gave Halstead's Bridge Street an unfamiliar look as a lorry was used to take people through the water up to the High Street. One brave soul decided to wade through in front of the Railway Hotel.

A look at the same floods from the other direction, at 9.50 a.m. according to the Co-op clock. The water is actually flowing out of Rosemary Lane like a river. All premises in the street suffered considerable damage from the two-day flood.

The last remains of the High Street Congregational church were demolished in the 1950s. The wall on the right stood for years as part of the Eastern National bus depot. All has now made way for Somerfields Superstore.

This is possibly the next day, as the front wall of the Manse, next to the church, is about to go. It was first mentioned in directories in 1832 when the minister was Revd Benjamin Johnson, who remained in office until around 1874, when Revd Peter Rutter took over.

The demise of the Swan Inn in the 1960s. For many years before it had been known as the Ship Inn, from where John Shadbolt used to run a freight business from the large workshop, which still stands at the back of the current Boots Chemists.

The steel framework for the new building is here seen under construction; it was originally Lipton's Supermarket until Boots moved in. The shops either side still stand. The lady walking up the street is Mrs Ardley who used to live in Paynters Terrace, Colne Road.

Even in wartime, film stars played their part in entertaining the troops. In this case it was Bing Crosby crooning to the men of the USAAF, the 381st Bomb Group at Ridgewell, which brought out many illicit cameras!

Also attending Ridgewell was Edward G. Robinson, before a B-17 Flying Fortress called *Stage Door Canteen*. He actually attended to 'christen' another aircraft, called *Happy Bottom*, named after his wife Gladys!

The unfortunate Kings Head, Colchester Road, which caught fire one Saturday lunchtime in the 1960s – the customers had to make a quick exit! The road was closed and all traffic diverted round Colne Road.

It was not long before the Kings Head reopened, but this time the thatched roof was replaced by tiles. The original Kings Head was demolished and replaced by the one above in 1937, but is now closed and has become a private house.

Again fire brings to an end of the life of a building, this time the barn that stood at the top of Tidings Hill, virtually at the junction with White Horse Avenue. It was possibly part of Highwoods estate, which in turn became a residential area.

Yet another piece of Halstead history bites the dust. This time it is the Manse of the Hedingham Road Baptist church, on the right, and two cottages on the left. The church itself suffered the same fate in recent years and was replaced.

Fifty years of Queen Victoria's reign were celebrated in 1887 when the fountain on the Market Hill was officially opened, certainly attracting a huge crowd. Note Felix Smith's harness and saddlery shop on the left with Elisha Sycamore's hardware store next door.

Another celebration, this time twenty-four years later, for the coronation of King George V, which seemed to attract a considerable military presence as well as the townsfolk.

Seven
At the Match

Halstead Free Church FC, 1911. From left to right, back row: Eb Norman, Willoughby Ellis, Bill Hardy, Ernie Cook, -?-. Centre row: Lew Rowland, Fred Mayes, Fred Hart, Archie Newton, Aubrey Wright. Front row: George Coe, Herb Sewell and Wally Cook.

Halstead CC before meeting Essex in the 1980s. From left to right, back row: Graham Mickley, Barry Root, John Hilliard, Mike James, Dave East and Peter Rawlinson (umpire). Front row: Terry Prestney, John Rice, Lloyd Rayner, Chris Webber and Alan Elsbury.

Holy Trinity School, *c.* 1953. From left to right, back row: Mr D. Leaming, Ray Osborne, Peter Blackwell, Phil Cook, John Slee, Billy Redman, Ralph Wilkin, Mr Clifford Jones (headmaster). Front row: Don Dowman, Robert Lake, Paul Root, Larry Plumb and Gerald Cook.

Halstead Tortoise Works CC, who played at Dooley Fields before the war. From left to right, back row: Charlie Britton, Jack Hardy, Terry Brown, Fred Brown, -?-, Bert Hart, Stan Gladwell. Front row: Eddie Alston, Gordon Sycamore, Ron Parr, 'Babe' Brown (scorer), 'Gas' Reeve and Bill Osborne.

Halstead Town FC, 1930. From left to right, back row: Charlie Conway, Fred Potter, Fred Amos, Jack Potter, Harold Bragg, Arthur Clark, George Abbott. Centre row: Ernie Mizon, Jack Hicks, Billy Welsh, Charlie Butler, Jack Cutting, Eb Norman, Charlie Sewell. Front row: Ernie Constable, John Curtis, Charlie Juniper, Jack Osborne and Charlie Whitfield.

Halstead CC, 1908. From left to right, back row: E. Harvey (umpire), Frank Reed Snr, F. Brown, ? Field, F. Sudbury, E. Baker, H. Norman. Centre row: 'Mun' Harvey, H. Cobb, Will Smith. Front row: F. Morley, Sol Weston and L. Brown.

Tortoise Works FC, 1927-28. From left to right, back row: Charlie Turner, Dick Kibble, Eddie Alston, Ollie Firmin, Stan Brazier, Percy Wright. Centre row: Billy Beckwith, Harold Bragg, Sid Bocking, Reg Spurgeon, Sid Brazier, Percy Root. Front row: Ted Taylor, Jack Osborne and Jimmy Plumb.

Courtauld's CC, 1900. From left to right, back row: Ted Dean, Albert Fry, A. Worsnop, John Charlton, Harry Whitehead, Albert Miller, Dick Hawkes, Abraham Newton. Front: Claude Myers, -?-, -?-, -?-, Jim Runtle, Percy Rayner and Jack Whitehead.

Courtauld's FC, c. 1964. From left to right, back row: Harold Smith, Jackie Holden, Roger Smith, Mick Goodey, Terry Rivers, Paul Root, Trevor Williams, Jack Osborne. Front row: Phil Cook, Norman Root, Dave Osborne, Geoff Steed, Paul Williamson and Geoff Brown.

Old Colonians FC, *c*. 1932. From left to right, back row: Mr Laing, Jack Squirrell, W. Hurry, W. Clover, C. Browne, E. Fluety, L. Lucas, George Root. Front row: Frank Palmer, J. Sycamore, John Curtis, Geoff Browne and Bob Laing.

St Andrew's FC, 1932-33. From left to right, back row: Mr Frank Vaizey, Charlie Wright, Frank Rayner, Bernard English, Eddie Barker. Centre row: Jack Edwards, Charlie Steed, Bert Brooks. Front row: Ken Hunt, Billy Edwards, Jack Mayes, Reg Argent, Geoff Rayner.

Courtauld's Bowls Club in the 1920s. From left to right, back row: Ernie Horwood, John Shaw, George Curtis, Barney Tuffin, John Curtis, Dick Basford. Centre row: John Smith, Ted Dean, George Thompson, Lou Widdop, Sam Pye, John Pearce, Charlie Goodwin. Front row: Bob Potts, Will Knowles, Bert Brewer, Wally May, Charlie Booth and Charlie Clements.

Gosfield Tennis Club, c. 1933. From left to right, back row: W. Bright, G. Baxter, Maurice Rowson. Centre row: Stan Randall, S. Dally, B. Piggin, Mrs E. Morgan, Miss E. Johnson, Mrs I. Francis, Revd A. Howe. Front row: R. McGregor, Mrs O. Haigh, Mrs T. Cresswell, Mrs W. Courtauld, Miss Betty Nuthall, Miss E. Harvey and A.R. French (secretary).

The Globe Inn darts team from Parsonage Street line up before a trip to the seaside in 1939. From left to right, back row: ? Dixey, Sid Diss, Frank Dines, Tom Mortimer, Ray Parmenter (half hidden), ? Howard, Perce Heavingham. Centre row: Alf Mortimer, 'Mac' Kibble, 'Tupenny' Kibble, -?-, George Bragg, ? Kibble, Len Rayner, Reg Potter, Mark Scillitoe (bus driver), Charlie Tilly. Seated: Bob Brett, Sam Turner, Walter 'Stumbler' Smith, 'Bonce' Kibble, Bob Mills and Cleveland Aldred.

Halstead Working Men's Club, champions of the Halstead Snooker League for four consecutive years from 1936-40. From left to right: Sam Kensall, Jack Bullard, Jack Coe, Eddie Steed, Stan Sach and Ken Broyd.

Eight
At the Photo Call

Halstead Co-operative Society management committee, 1930. From left to right, back row: J. Cooper, J. Moules, G. Clarke (North Street), Sam Pye, Ted Parker. Front row: W. Beadle, Mrs Plaistow, W. Spurgeon, H. Rayner, S. Francis, Mrs Hayward and G. Clarke (Beridge Road).

Halstead Working Men's Club committee *c.* 1938. From left to right, back row: Alf Edwards, George Deal, Fred Johnson, Frank Harrington, Wally Pilgrim. Centre row: Bert Tansley, Jimmy Springett, Bert Owers, Ronald Long (legal adviser), Eddie Steed, Claud Reeve, Jack Bullard. Front row: Mike Bearman, Harry Layzell, Mr Steel (CIU), Len Spurgeon, Charlie Ready, Mr Thompson (CIU), Lou Widdop, Sam Kensall and George Downs.

St Andrew's Mothers' Union, *c.* 1914. From left to right, back row: Revd Thomas Curling, his aunt, Mrs Cadby, Miss Hornor, Mesdames Harvey, Mayes, Curling, Bearman, Edwards, Snowden, Miss Hartle, Mrs Chamberlain, Revd Chamberlain, Mesdames Mells, Gardiner, Amos, Brown, Fincham, Bess, Plaistow, Parmenter, Coe, Norman and Arnold. Children sitting: Mrs Amos' grand-daughter, Revd Chamberlain's son and Revd Curling's son.

Samuel Courtauld's Works Council, *c.* 1960. From left to right, back row: Tom Galley, ? Hartley, Frank Smith, Hazel Bragg, Ray Baker, ? Wheater, Eric Radford, Dorothy Wade. Centre row: Rose Rayner, Kathy Whipps, Bert Mumford, Flo Rayner, Tom Copling. Seated: Bernard Hunt and Sheila Scillitoe.

St Andrew's choir in the 1920s. From left to right, back row: Bert Meadows, Wally Miller, Claude Snowdon, Douglas Brookes, Alf Suckling, Claude Byford, Bert Evans. Centre: Basil Newton, Fred Miller, Hubert Goodram, Frank Vaizey, Percy Charrington, Alf Wicker, Stan Lucas. Front row: Don Danby, Louis Woods, Charlie Stubbings, Fred Suckling and Jim Suckling.

St Andrew's Boys' Club, *c.* 1936. From left to right, back row: -?-, Len Spurgeon, Wally Brown, Alan Coe, Reg Gowers, Gerald Goodey, Ken Turp. Second row: Fred Edwards, Denis Parmenter, Don Hume, Tom Finch, Jack Curtis, Keith Kingston, Eric Radford, Ted Willis, Ken Blower, Ted Bearman, Sid Nicholls, Francis Knowles, Arthur Edwards, Harry Cook. Third row: ? Pilgrim, Don Fairhead, Revd Alan Swallow, Eddie Evans, Frank Vaizey, Arthur Barrett, Rex Hardy, Alf Wicker, John Barge, Peter Darling, Joe Miller. Front row: -?-, -?-, Wally Cocksedge, Lenny Britton, Bernie Downs, Jeff Barry, Ray Gibbs, Clive Runtle, Ken Ward, Jim Davey, Eddie Turner, Jack Howard, ? Coe and Ray Collier.

Halstead Working Men's Club committee and officers, 1952. From left to right, back row: P. Wicker, C. Smith, Fred Root, C. Coe, Jack Downs, Billy Smith, Don Cook, George Lee, Wally Pilgrim. Front row: Bert Lock, Jack Wade, George Downs, Ernie Wordsworth, F. Castle and Alf Edwards.

Halstead Guides, 1924. From left to right, back row: Mary Norfolk, Flo Reeve, Miss Ada Davey, Ivy Harrington. Second row: Ivy Arnold, Doreen Constable, Winnie Reynolds, Violet Abbott, Ena Button, -?-, Dora Wicker, Connie Baker. Third row: Cissie Abbott, Gwen Firmin, Ivy Clift, Winnie Edwards, Nora Wicker, ? Clark , -?-, ? Arnold. Third row: Hilda Snowden, Edna Kibble, Nora Curtis, Rose Edwards, Mrs Saunders, ? Binks, Eva Tansley, Lennox Kibble. Front row: Ivy Cooper, Doris Burl, ? Cooper and Milly Burl.

Halstead Working Men's Club committee, c. 1924. From left to right, back row: B. Wilkin, H. Alston, Lou Widdop, J. Moal, J. Arnold, George Hardy, George Reynolds. Centre row: S. King, Len Spurgeon, Charlie Ready, Harry Layzell, Aubrey Wright, George Lawrence. Front row: W. Goodey, Sam Kensall, Fred Suckling and Alec Yerbury.

Halstead's 'City Fathers' outside their union offices in Colchester Road in the 1920s; the building is now used as a clinic. From left to right, back row: F. Bishop, S. Philp, F. Hunt, Revd Arthur Curling. Second: D. Unwin, A. Mann, T. Bell, J. Jackson, E. Doubleday, J. Porkess, Revd B. Cann, A. Metson, L. Delf, T. Goodchild, E. Parker, Canon Lampen, B. May, A. Gardiner, J. Kirkwood, E. Knight. Front row: J. Nott, H. Hills, Mrs Vaizey, Miss Hornor, R. Vaizey, T. Whitlock, S. Long, A. Blomfield, F. Vaizey.

The late Enoch Powell MP was guest of honour at a Halstead Local History Society meeting, when he gave a talk on the Bourchier family. This was followed by a reception in the White Hart, with, from left to right: Revd Paul Angwin, Geoffrey Copsey, Roy McDowell, Sir Ronald Long, Mr Powell, Lady Long. Seated: Joan McDowell and Laura Copsey.

Halstead Wolf Cubs around 1918. Included are: Charlie Juniper, Alan Spurgeon, Jack Osborne, Sid Bocking, Freddie Backler, Lew Porter, Frank Smith, Tom Mayes, Ted Suckling, Freddie Constable, Ted Williamson, Basil Randall, Herschel Kibble, Bob Rayner, Bert Goodrum, Joe Miller, Arthur Bugbee, Bob Goward and George Abbott.

This establishment is rather a mystery, possibly something to do with St Andrew's church, with a collection of musical instruments around the early years of the century. Among those involved are: Ted Parker, Sid Simmons, George Hardy, Aubrey Wright, 'Mun' Harvey and Percy Bush. Ideas from readers would be most welcome.

Members of the management committee of the Foresters' Court Pride of Halstead at their centenary dinner. From left to right: Clive Hall, Peggy Arnold, Fred Humphries, Bill David, Fred Brown, Chief Ranger C.A. Minchin (behind), Roy Giller, Charlie Juniper.

Nine
Along the Colne Valley

Looking up Swan Street towards Halstead, the children are again out to see what the photographer is up to. They are standing outside the Bell public house, now closed and converted to a private residence. Note the shop on the right, now demolished.

Castle Hedingham this time, looking down St James' Street, with the Bell on the left, a one-time court-house. At the far end stood Hedingham House, then a shop and home of Fred Hawkins, the local wheelwright.

Looking in the other direction towards Sudbury back in the 1920s. There is not a car in sight and the two lads can stand in the road. There was a great variety of shops in St James Street in those days, when people lived, worked and shopped in the village.

In the spring the River Colne is fast moving at Castle Hedingham bridge, but by the autumn has slowed down to a gentle, peaceful trickle. The bridge was built in 1736 by Robert Poole according to the tablet in the brickwork, to connect the two Hedinghams.

It's a long time since the Eleven Elms at Crouch Green, Castle Hedingham, looked like this – a real rural local, with the lane winding up to the village. Back in the 1970s it ceased to be a pub and became a night spot, called Memories; the garden to the right is now the car park.

Castle Hedingham FC, 1926. From left to right, back row: Tucker Ripper (president), Arthur King, Jack Borthwick, Reg Rayner, Ashley Ripper, W. Davidson, Silas Smee, Reg Staines, Jack Drury, Jack Leathers, Harry Ripper, Jack Coates. Front row: Ernie Smee, Steve Toole and Charlie Butler.

The weather, as usual, was unpredictable, and one May in the 1970s a sudden downpour flooded Alderford Street in Sible Hedingham and householders peered out anxiously from behind sandbags as council workmen tried to clear blocked drains.

Along the road at Great Yeldham stood a famous oak. Local legend has it that it was once part of Epping Forest that stretched up into East Anglia. This picture looking towards Ridgewell was taken in 1912 from Stonebridge Meadow, which has since been built over.

Just round the corner was the village green where the row of cottages still stands, as does the shop on the left, on the Tilbury road. Darkin's Stores is yet to be built on the road to the right, which winds its way up to Little Yeldham.

In rural villages, it was a normal sight to see milk being delivered from a pony and trap, and here the milkmaid Mary Bride, of D.B. Rose of Hill Farm, is busy on her rounds in Ridgewell. It must have been in quieter days with the transport right across the road!

Toppesfield FC once played Halstead Town twice in a day in 1946. Included are: Bill Smith, Humphrey Smith, Sir Leslie Plummer, Les Kemp, Fred Kemp, Alf Hardy, Vic Clark, Wally Beadle, F. St G. Unwin, Harold Goodchild, Frank Nash, Bob Castle, Bill Robert, Humphrey Roberts, Cliff Hardy, Tom Pannell, ? Lawrence, Dick Ruggles, John Peat, 'Nobby' Clark, Jack Boreham, Aubrey Dace and Jack Babbage.

Gosfield Hall just after the First World War was a busy place for the Rowe family in terms of employees. From left to right, back row: Edward Everitt, May Scrivener, Horace Reeve, Ethel Hunt, George Baxter, Edith Ambrose, Ted Jarman, Daisy Foster, Tom Hutchin. Second row: Jim Rowson, Ellen Barker, Miss Hodson, Miss Mills, Grace Gurney, Flo Moore. Front: Charlie Robinson and Will Tobias.

Again the photographer of the day attracted people out in Gosfield at the turn of the century judging by the number of bicycles! This is outside the old post office, which has now moved to the last building on the left in the picture, with the Green Man next door, on the right.

A peaceful scene in Ox Yard, Gosfield, just after the First World War. It was a favourite stopping place for drivers to rest their livestock en route to and from Braintree market, when there were no cattle floats.

Gosfield FC, 1925. From left to right, back row: Charlie Robinson, Gerald Owers, Arthur Jeggo, Aubrey Smith, Frank Owers, Bill Bright, Arthur Watts, Bob Britton, Horace Reeve. Second row: Eric Owers, Percy Jeggo, Dick Tobias, George Baxter. Front row: Ernie Barker, Maurice Rowson, Herbert Heavingham, Claude Humphries and George Anderson.

A couple of lads met the photographer in The Street, Pebmarsh. The little shop on the end of the cottages on the right was believed to be a branch of E. & B. Smith, saddlers of Halstead. The house on the left still stands, but the one in the centre has gone.

An idyllic setting for these cottages in Fox Road, Wickham St Paul, before the last war. The thatched building on the right is called Rosedene, was once actually two homes, while those on the left were in fact four, which were demolished in the early 1950s.

At the other end of the Colne Valley builders are at work constructing the bridge in Chappel in 1905, when scaffolding looked rather scarce! The only recognizable building is Watch House, which still dominates the crossroads.

A scene from yesteryear when these cottages at Wakes Colne stood in front of the parish church, next to the old school, first a blacksmith's and now an engineering business. Pictured from left to right: Mesdames -?-, Wendon, Leatherdale, Patten, Wright and Alice Root.

This pair of cottages used to stand on White Colne Green beside the very busy Halstead-Colchester Road. They were demolished many years ago, the back gardens used as allotments. Then these disappeared and the site is now a complete village green.

Further down the hill was Colne Ford across the River Colne. The bridge, built in the 1890s, was rebuilt in the 1990s, while the ford crossing has long gone. Note the house in the background which was once a pub, The White Hart.

Celebrating the end of the last war at Earls Colne George, now The Coachman, with Ginger's Brass Band. From left to right, back row: John Sumner, Major Phillips, Percy Warren, Billy Poulter Jnr, Peter Willingham, Bob Matthews. Centre row: 'Ginger' Sumner, Mrs Dawson, George Boar, Jack Whittle, Reg Bragg, 'Doddie' Wass, Dave Dawson (landlord). Front row: Bill Reear, Bill Poulter Snr, Jim Pratt and Mrs Scillitoe.

Colne Engaine School pupils line up in 1908. From left to right, back row: Ralph Alliston, Arthur Partridge, Frank Proctor, ? Coppin, Mr H.E. Smith (headmaster), Percy Wakeling, -?-, W. Gardiner, George Mann, W. Brewer. Second row: ? Copping, Minnie Partridge, Emily Cambrrok, Beatrice Potter, -?-, Fred Gilbert, George Wright, Harry Gilbert. Third row: Florrie Johnson, Alice Hicks, -?-, ? Brewer, Dorothy Gilbert, ? Brewer, Stella Smith, Kate Partridge. Front: William Gilbert, ? Whybrow, ? Cambrook, -?-, D. Brewer, -?-, ? Gardiner, ? Cockerton.

The meeting of two modes of transport, with an early motorcycle and a horse and buggy outside The Lion in Earls Colne High Street. Presumably the owner of the bike in front of the horse is wetting his whistle inside!

Lower down the street was the place to catch the bus to Colchester, just past Queens Road. This was one of Blackwell's earliest with solid tyres and open top, but driver Tom Simmons did not have to bother with the weather.

It's time for an outing from Greenstead Green when the members of the parish church line up before their big day out probably to the coast by train from Halstead, all dressed up in their Sunday best. Can anyone be recognized?

In the past Greenstead Green did have its less affluent quarters as these cottages show, now long demolished. They were possibly for the workers at the village windmill, which is itself only a memory but played an important part in village life years ago.

126

The bottom of Grange Hill, Greenstead Green, in 1908 looks far different from today. In those days there were ten Saunders children in the village and most of them are here. From left to right: -?-, Albert, Edie (on stone), Daisy, Nellie, Ernie and Arthur. Lucy, Bertha and Dorothy were missing.

Greenstead Green FC, 1948. From left to right, back row: Arthur Rayner, John Sexton, Jim Sibley, John Quick, Harry Marshall, Jack Evans, Stan Eley, Len Cook. Centre row: Ted Secker, Ron Rayner, Roy Salmon, Arthur Hume, Dave Root. Front row: Keith Rippingale and Dennis Walford.

A far cry from the crowded High Street of today, when there was time to have a wander: this view is from around the turn of the century. Note the tiled barrel arch on the left of the road which contains the original ditch that runs down the hill from Paynters Pond in Head Street to the River Colne beside the bridge.